MF /2 79

UNDER THE SHADE OF A TREE

Sue

Best wishes

Rissa

Sooo

UNDER THE SHADE OF A TREE

SOMALI WOMEN SPEAK

PUBLISHED BY TRAUMA AWARENESS

First published in Great Britain in 2018,
by Trauma Awareness, Bristol, U.K.

© Text copyright Rissa Mohabir.
© Images copyright Bridget O'Brien.

Editing and design by Jack Challoner.

ISBN: 978-1-9996772-0-6

Acknowledgements

I wish to thank the following people for
helping to make this book possible.

The narrators: Soad Ali Hassan, Fatima,
Hodan, Asha Noor, Obah, Muna, Saada,
Medina, Liin, Ayan, and Amina.

Also Layla Ismail for her written contributions.

For support in kind: Sarah Dailly
(Barton Hill Settlement), Den Carter
and Imogen McIntosh for fundraising.

Also thanks to Bridget O'Brien (artist) and to
Jack Challoner (editor and designer) for their
enthusiasm and expertise, and of course to
my family and friends for
their encouragement.

Rissa.

My Mother Tongue
Rich and full of wonders.
Words with rhythm,
Proverbs that express
Feelings and frustrations,
Joys and Love.

Here I am
speaking in a foreign language,
Lost for words and in
many ways so frustrated.
Poems, poetries and songs
keep my language and hope alive.
Oh! My dear mother tongue.

Layla Ismail

Contents

Introduction

by Rissa Mohabir,
Founder and Director of Trauma Awareness.

This book contains narrative prose written by women from Somalia who had found refuge and sanctuary in Bristol, U.K. The origins of this project come from my experience in the psychology of trauma, which I have gained over thirty years.

The Trauma Awareness perspective emerged when I was working in Serbia and Croatia post-conflict as a visiting trainer and homeopath to medical doctors, just after the bombing of Belgrade (2000 to 2007). I was primarily involved with paediatricians and medical doctors as part of a training team, where civilians on both sides had endured the horrors of war, significant loss of family members and extreme conditions. Anyone with experience of post-genocide conflict will have some understanding on how this impacts on the individual and the society.

I spent seven years listening to stories alongside a medical team who had themselves been exposed to these extreme experiences. I was aware that there was an elephant in the room: post-traumatic stress disorder (PTSD).

It was not until 1980 that PTSD was officially classified (in the third edition of the American Psychiatric Association's Diagnostic and

Statistical Manual, DSM-III). PTSD is a condition in which a person constantly experiences fear, helplessness or horror – a feeling that their life is under threat. It results from traumatic experiences, which can include witnessing or being confronted by death or serious injury.

It became apparent to me that this information had not cascaded out to mental health and trauma services.

After an intense period working in a post-conflict region, I took what was meant to be a much needed sabbatical in 2009, that later shaped the next chapter of my work. My interest in body-mind studies became focussed on trauma at the Somatic Experiencing Trauma Institute in New York. The Founder, Peter Levine, has made a significant contribution to the classification and diagnosis of PTSD, alongside his contemporaries and colleagues. It is their view that 'trauma is not about the event but our individual response to the impact on mind and body'.

Hence my reason for providing Trauma Awareness Training as a valuable resource to the first responders, support workers, volunteers and other personnel working in the trauma related field.

The studies became articulated over thirty years of observation and insights in clinical practice. I no longer wished to gather survivors' stories only for them to be later locked away in filing cabinets. I realised that supporting service providers with basic concepts and skills through trauma training was part of the bigger picture of listening projects, which I will describe later.

It is no surprise that there is a compelling need to support those who support others in the trauma services. I was fortunate to have had the privilege to pilot my training program with Barnardos (South Gloucestershire, UK) and the NHS helpline (in nearby Bristol), designed as a first-aid approach on how to understand and identify the noticeable signs of a trauma response.

I returned to Bristol in 2011. This could not have been more timely, as it coincided with Bristol becoming a City of Sanctuary. This meant Bristol City Council, multi-faith groups, refugee services and schools undertook the pledge to welcome those who flee because of threat to life or persecution from their original country of conflict. City of Sanctuary is now a growing movement with a network of cities nationwide.

My quest to understand the impact of war on women was shaped by the impressions and stories from the women in Serbia and Croatia; haunting images of distress and distrust that they shared in the process of picking up the pieces of their shattered lives. That is the harsh reality of post-conflict situations. I decided it was time to start listening to the lived experiences on the impact of war on women.

My direction was determined. I wanted to provide safe spaces for refugee women from the Bristol community and beyond, where many of them they had never found their voice, had not been heard. What evolved was a need to provide listening projects. Time and time again I would hear the phrase "We're bursting with stories".

I realised I was stepping onto a new terrain of community listening, of building trust with those who have a story to tell. What took me by surprise — and it shouldn't have really — was that trust was gained because the Listening Project was presented under the umbrella of Trauma Awareness. Throughout the process I applied the key concepts from my guide: HOPE (safe listening for trauma narratives).

Holding
Orientation
Pacing the narrative
Engagement

Someone was willing to listen to the painful memories of what made these women seek sanctuary here in Bristol. What emerged is that the women participated because their stories would provide a service for the wider community. Implicit in safe listening is the need to pace a narrative to avoid overwhelming the narrator. Finding a place in the circle is vital preparation for going back in time, to enable memories to percolate to the surface.

This is a huge shift away from individualistic cultures. I was embarking on new ground, with women from collectivist cultures, who see themselves as 'we' rather than 'me'. They feel secure sitting in a circle and sharing with a sense of purpose. And this is what led to *Under the Shade of the Tree – Somali Women Speak*.

I hope their narratives capture this selfless act of giving truthful experience without analysis. The group narratives took on the form of a one voice project, the narrators remembering together, like an echo chamber, their words woven together, amplifying painful and harrowing memories, insights, wisdom, resilience and resources.

Some of the women retained their privacy for reasons that need no explanation; within the refugee community, that is a given. The key is listening to oneself, listening to others and being listened to. That is part of the process of healing stories, the simple act of speaking and listening.

The Somali women from the refugee community agreed due to cultural considerations of their Muslim faith that they would retain their privacy with no photographs, social media, recording or filming to document the process.

We agreed that their words would be written by a scribe and decisions about what remained and what would be shared would be a collaborative process.

I cannot stress enough how important laughter, coffee and croissants, and finding a place in the circle, were as preparation for going back in time, or for some to where they were "stuck in time", to enable memories to percolate to the surface. Implicit in safe listening is the need to pace a narrative to avoid overwhelm.

As Richard Mollica describes in his 2008 book Healing Invisible Wounds: "If we go too directly, it's like looking at the blinding sun". Instead, to assist the storyteller, he encourages "A little bit, a lot over a period of time".

Rissa Mohabir, 2018.

This introduction was derived from a conversation with Dr. D-M Withers, Research Fellow at the University of Sussex, researching the histories of feminist publishing.

Under the Shade of a Tree ...

We gathered in groups
Families and strangers
Sleeping and resting under the trees
On our journeys
Fleeing to safety
After the war had started ...   7

Soft Heart,
We Don't Like Violence

First the mum, mum, mum then father.
Power of mother's love.

Soft Heart,
We Don't Like Violence

It's inhuman to keep killing without reason
A lorry carries seventy civilians at night
Grenades and guns everywhere
Bodies everywhere.

Shelter in the stables
A farmer helps compress
her mother's wound on her neck
Bleeding, she protects and covers
her daughter from shooting and rape
The power of a mother's love.

Soft heart, we don't like violence.

Years later the bullet is removed
Though metal still remains in her body
Beeping at airports
Burning in the heat of the sun

Soft heart, we don't like violence.

Hodan's Story

A memory of Somalia

It's morning, and on waking I make canjeero,
My sisters go to work, my brother is at University.
Each morning I go outside, talking to neighbours.

Daytime is very hot but after the clouds burst
the water flows,
Children run and play in the rain.
Then the sun comes out again.

It's so beautiful, I smell the flowers.
The air is fresh and clean,
It's so beautiful.

My experience

When I was 16 or 17 (in 2001) the shooting in Mogadishu started. I was so frightened; I remember covering my face with my shawl so as not to see what the soldiers were doing.

We all decided to run to a village away from the shooting, thinking that we would be returning the next day so we just left with what we were wearing. Many of our family were lost.

The situation was terrible, and we had hardly any food, hardly any drink.

As we tried to escape, a soldier shot me on my buttock. I lay very still, numb with shock and so scared, and I couldn't cry. I have never cried since then about that memory.

I had a big swelling on my foot, couldn't walk and the pain was everywhere. My sister and I used shawls wrapped as bandage, and with a stick I was able to hop.

During the war, the hospitals were giving us free antibiotic injections to help prevent wound infection. I think this helped me.

We hid in a banana orchard waiting to hear if the fighting had stopped. There were hundreds of people running for safety. The news was bad. We knew we would not be going back the next day. My brother took the risk to return to our home and collect our I.D. papers, money but everything else was left behind. I remember my gold jewellery, my clothes, everything about our home gone. It's so sad.

I started to feel there was no sense of time though the sharp pain was spreading from my leg to shoulder.

Finally we managed to get a lift to Ethiopia, three days of driving where other Somali families looked after us when we arrived. The doctors took out my bullet, it was about 2 inches long, but after that weakness in my leg left my foot floppy and curled inwards. I was told it was because the nerve had been cut.

After lots of calls to England, we finally boarded a plane for England in 2002 to join family as an asylum seeker. On arrival we were taken to a hostel as a new arrival to get our papers sorted. We were in a hostel for one year before we were sent to Bristol, where my new life began.

What helps me go on?

Faith and prayer helps;
Helps me to forget everything.
Inshallah. Prayer is like a support inside
Makes my mind feel stronger.

I am telling my story
But I don't want to go inside the story
So I choose where to go to remember.
Prayer helps to forget.
Prayer helps to ease the memory.

Memories of our country

All the clans lived in harmony
As a community.

Every Friday we met,
Men, women and children
To watch and take part in traditional dances
Going to the national theatre and cinema.
Let's hold on to our memories of peace time.

As a community ...
Every Saturday
We went to the beach
For picnics and rest.

As a community ...
Looking out for one another,
When a baby is born in Somalia,
The neighbours looked after
Mother and child.

Liin, Medina and Saada

Community to Conflict

Shotguns, grenades,
Knives and guns.
Rebels came to the city.
You can't help your brother,
You can't help your neighbour,
You can only help yourself.

Saada's Story

I tell this story so that when I die,
something will be left,
I carry my injuries with me every day,
on my body and inside of me.

When the night sky was red and blue
with explosions and gunshots,
There was dust and smoke everywhere.
Everyone tried to run to survive.

A huge explosion and then bleeding like rain.
Could feel the pain all over, so fast so quick.
Shrapnel entered my body.
My eyes swollen from the bullet wound
I couldn't see for two weeks.

In that moment, my life exploded,
There was blood everywhere,
Then I realised my fingers were no more.

I am carrying the scars and memories
all the time.

It makes me sad every day.
I am sad.

It's agony
Carrying metal in the body
Like small bits of corn moving around
Especially, in the cold winter.

Nobody ever asks what happened in the war.

Nobody ever asks what happened to my fingers.

A lot of people have shrapnel and bullets
In their bodies.
A lot of people have many memories.
It's an untold story.
It's a secret.

Medina, Liin, Saada.

Explosions, shrapnel
Injured my knee,
Many years later,
Still swollen with pain
Worse at night,
Worse in heat and cold.

Medina

The soldiers came.
Men and boys taken away,
Stripped.
Women screamed.
Women wailed.

Amina

So many people raped.
War does this.

Saada

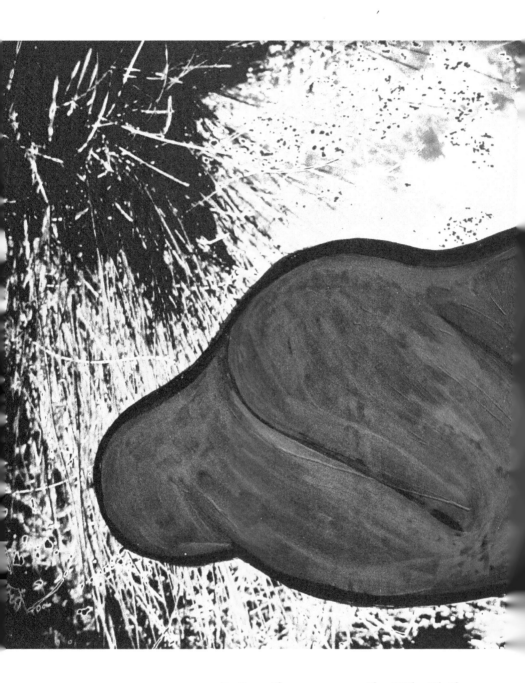

Mother and Child

*As a mother, I had to keep strong
for the children.*

As a mother, I had to keep strong
for the children,
To keep the homesick feelings inside.
Not to let the children see my sadness.

I used to ask
"Why is every door closed?
Where are the people?
Only an umbrella, coat and head down."

I used to think
"No one knows Fatima.
Only the postman."
That's loneliness.

I prayed to Allah to keep my faith strong.
I would be lost if I went down,
Everything would collapse.

Many years later.
What goes around, comes around.
Listening to new arrivals, asylum seekers
Translating in Arabic and Somali.

Speaking from the heart.
We are all human beings,
Beyond nation, creed, colour or religion.
We are all of the same humanity.

Fatima

Fatima's Story

A memory of Hargeisa

Life was simple and safe
The doors of our homes always open,
Where neighbours helped one another
Looking after the children.

The daily routine of our lives,
Everyone is outside, cooking on charcoal stoves,
In the heat of the midday sun
We eat, rest and sleep.
It's so peaceful.

My experience

In August 1988, we escaped from Hargeisa as the shooting got closer. We didn't have a car, so with my one-year-old daughter, we joined others fleeing, the elderly men, mainly farmers, and women, mothers, children; about eighty families headed towards Ethiopia.

There were car loads of people rushing by, lots of shouting and people dying around us. I had no choice before we ran, as we could hear the gunshots.

We walked for a month, miles and miles across savannah and mountains, sandy slopes; my feet were swollen, bleeding and blistered, carrying my child.

I was so scared I didn't feel anything, not even hunger or tiredness, hard to describe but this strange feeling like in labour when it's all about survival. I had this sense of deep shock where keeping awake day and night could help me to survive.

Separated ...

Age thirteen in hospital from injury,
My mother in another hospital, far away.
We lost one another.
We did not reunite for many years.

Saada

When the bombs came
My mum and son age eighteen months
Ran to survive,
We didn't find each other for two months.

Liin

Ayan's Story

A memory of Hargeisa

As a child
Life was fun.
I loved playing football with my friends.

We lived in the City.
But every Friday we went to the seaside
With family and friends.

My experience

I was only seven years old when the war started. I remember the sky looked red with bombing. I was so scared. Dad and Mum took our clothes and we walked in the night to keep safe.

Aeroplanes were bombing above us. I saw many people die. My first cousin, aged twenty, was disabled from the injuries, and that made me sad.

One night, I got separated from my Mum and Dad. I was crying for them, lost and frightened. Another parent looked after me. My Mum risked the bombing to come looking for me.

This happened again with my father and another time my brother was lost. We found one another after searching.

What helps me go on?

> The memory feels long ago
> If someone reminds me
> Or if I see stories on the TV
> I feel sadness.
>
> It's a long time ago.
> I am alive.
> I am okay.

Crossing Over

Muna's Story

Memory in Peace Time (age 10)
Dubai: The City of Alin

My Home
Life was a joy
In the early morning, my daily routine
Woken by the sounds of the chickens
The smell of breakfast of laxoox with spiced tea
Prepared by my mother,
Before going to school.

The doors were always open.
Friends running, playing together,
And from our window
Our neighbour's camels and goats
Walked by on the fine sandy ground.
Life was a joy.

My experience

At the age of ten, in 1991, my father suddenly died of a heart attack. Life changed as we couldn't live in the house and the government said we all had to leave Dubai and return to Somaliland but the war meant it wasn't safe to return.

My grandfather saved us by looking after us, but financially the situation was difficult for my mother as a widow. Then my grandfather died, so when I was fifteen, my mother decided to move to Europe to save us and have a better life.

It was sudden. I didn't have time to say goodbye to my friends, as plans were made to meet a man to help us get across Europe with documents.

The experience was challenging, as we flew from Dubai to Syria, and in my mind kept wondering where we were going. From then it became scary. The house was cold, with no heating, or running water. My mother had packed food to carry on the journey.

For two months, we had to learn to say new names and dates of birth if stopped. The man took us on a train and we headed for Portugal. We waited in train stations for hours, then on to another train to Spain and then more waiting before another one to Paris, and our final destination, the Netherlands.

The man left us there and it was then we realised we were meant to look like his family with false passports.

Refugee Camp: Ocdorenta, The Netherlands.
We were living in a big tent on a field, queuing three times a day for food that we had not eaten before. I missed the flat bread and halal meat and our last meal was at 5 pm.

Everything was so different, and in the beginning there wasn't anyone with our dialect. We lived like this for five months, and still I kept asking 'what next'?

We moved to another place for two years and then suddenly once again we had to leave, as without the correct papers we were told we would have to go back to Somaliland, which was still at war. This time, I travelled with two women, and now realise I was trafficked, pretending to be one of their family.

Finally we were safe, as asylum seekers in the U.K. to begin a new life.

Bristol
Our asylum was granted with leave to remain and eventually I became a British citizen. I feel safe here as we have a big Somali community. I feel as if I have not lost my culture, religion, language and food.

Now I am married with children, I realise what my mother did to get us to a safe place. My daily routine of waking to the sounds of the city of Bristol, my past forever changed.

What keeps me going?

The sadness is not forgotten
Suddenly leaving my homeland,
Remembering the journey and hard times
That we went through.

Faith makes me hopeful,
Starting over again
I keep going
To learn
A new life, a new language
A new culture.

Soad's Story

A Route to a Better Future
(1992-2000)

The War in Somalia,
Meant no return for Somalis from Kuwait,
My mother and we four sisters boarded
a flight to Turkey,
Then a bus to Syria.
Across mountains, through valleys and villages.

A flight to Moscow, a cold Russian city.
We arrived frozen, with no coats, wearing sandals.
Six months, waiting for passports.
Changed my identity
No more Soad,
My name was now Maria from Guatemala.

At the age seventeen with my cousin,
First time away from my mother and sisters,
We crossed the border to Poland
And on to Germany where we rested
With a Somali family from our clan.

I returned to being Soad Ali
To cross the border to the Netherlands,
Another place of refuge with a family
For one month
Before moving to a Refugee Camp.

We waited with no news.
I waited six months for my sister to arrive
with family reunion services tracing us.
I waited two years for my mother and little sister.

A new life begun, new language, marriage with child.
Our papers in order,
we finally joined our brother in the U.K.

Obah's Story

Memory of Peace Time
Kuwait

New Beginnings
My first year in secondary school
A change in life
Excited to learn
Curious.

New Beginnings
Becoming independent
Building my future
With
Dreams and ambitions
To be a doctor of medicine.

My Experience

Everything changed when the Gulf War started in 1990.

Moscow
With my mother and sisters we left looking for a safe place and headed for Moscow and then on to Europe.

My eldest sister left first towards the Netherlands. We had no news or calls from her.

Six months later, at the age of seventeen, I set off with a cousin and a group of men and women, walking over the mountains through Germany and on to the border of the Netherlands.

Even now I can remember the smell of snow in the freezing cold and on our journey we hid in basements, hungry with no food. The only way to keep going was to say that we were heading somewhere, just anywhere in Europe to be safe and live in peace.

My mind tries to rub off these bad memories.

The Netherlands

At the border of the Netherlands, I was taken to a camp where they traced my sister in another camp. That memory of seeing her again is hard to describe.

We were resettled to a small town Kerkrade on the border of Germany with only three other Somali families. Living there was a lonely time as the culture and language was too different. By then I was married with children and after nine years once again we were on the move with my family, my mother and sisters to join my brother in England.

Bristol

When we moved to Bristol in 2000 there were only a few Somali families but over the years, many more Somalian families from across Europe reunited to live in Bristol.

Our new life began, and from there on the family stay together.

What kept me going?

The first thing
My belief tells me to be patient and keep going.

My mother is an example
Her advice always to keep strong
Like a tree
No matter how hard the wind blows
Like a tree
She never falls.

I am
Picking up the pieces
When the war delayed
Early dreams and ambitions.

I've done my duty as a mother
The children are in education.
Now it's my time
To do something in life
Study and gain qualifications.

I have an aim, I have a goal,
I will persevere.

Under the Shade of a Tree

We tell our stories
Twenty-five years later.

I remember ...
We were lucky, there was rain
To make tea in the Nido milk tin.
Sometimes we would find rice.

I remember ...
Fear and worry for missing family
Made me leave the tree, against all advice
To find them in the city
Where the soldiers hid in trees and streets.

I remember ...
After I was shot and couldn't walk
I had a stick and a bandage
to help me leave the city.
"Please help me," I called.
But everywhere was fighting and shooting.

With my stick for support
And a bandage to lift my foot
I found my way, a car going to my home
But the driver left me on the side ofthe road
In the middle of nowhere.

I remember ...
My passport, my I.D. is my safety
Without it I am lost in the war.
My mother went back to find my passport
So we could escape to Ethiopia.

I came to by chance, from a peaceful place.
I carried my children, I worried for them always,

Frightened in this place with nothing.

Sometimes we slept on the ground.

It was quiet and we felt safe.
But in the night, the aeroplanes came and shot at us.
The mother and baby beside me died.

On the journey we used sticks as toothbrushes.
Sometimes we didn't wash, and our bodies shut down.

I remember....
I left with my four daughters and only a handbag.
I couldn't bring my medicines.

Two years on the way to safety.
Cold Russian cities, unwelcomed
Alone as Mum and Dad, I was sad.

With no language or medicine.
We made our way slowly, with pain.

I remember, I remember, I remember, I remember ...
How our faith helped us to forget the stories
that make up our journeys to safety.

Remembering and listening now,
We are unwinding the bandage
That covered our wounds.

Under the shade of the tree
We gather again, strong in our faith
Vulnerable in our memories
Sharing our stories to heal
And feel lighter on our ways.

One day we will write the stories for our children.

Reflections ...

We hope
Other refugee women
Will open up and talk,
Will come out of their houses.

We hope
Others will know
What has happened to us.
And all women in war.

We hope
To break barriers,
To stop being asked
"When are you going back?"

We have peace
We have life.

Afterwords ...

1. *Layla Ismail*

Development manager, Refugee Women of Bristol.

Under the Shade of a Tree – Somali Women Speak is symbolic of a long held tradition of Somali society. It is in the art of oral poetry and song that remains a vital part of Somali culture for women.

All my life was poetry. As a child, mothers sang the lullaby that we later learnt and passed on. My grandfather and uncle were poets. Some are more gifted as poets but language and literacy is heavily based on recitation and also knowing the meaning.

Almost like Shakespeare studies from year 6 class I remember we had to seek elders, sitting under the shade of the tree, to help translate meaning and metaphor about Aloe Vera, the succulent plant. They compared how the bitter sap and the sweet honey in the flower is like two families having differences and yet coexisting. Or another way of thinking about it is that even when a person has bitterness there is always a sweet part on the inside.

To illustrate communal society meeting under the shade of the tree, men express through a style known as Gabay and Geeraar and women as Buraambur in the style of dance and oral poetry. For example, people communicate through marriage by exchanging poetry to the clans.

Capturing frustrations with no written word in our culture until 1972. The only way to convey messages was a direct expression through recitation. The tradition of proverbs still lives on in everyday speech, the message passed on from previous generations. For example, if someone is going too slowly, we say "Are you killing an elephant with a needle?" Another one is "Learn from someone, and then you are cleverer".

Oral poetry is direct and not complex, though our language is complicated with rhythms and repetition. Our greatest fear is that our children are missing out on the richness or our language.

2. *Soad Ali Hassan*
Co-producer of the Somali Listening Project.

I met Rissa Mohabir at a committee meeting for International Women's Day in 2012, where she invited me to take part in a listening project, *Through the Eyes of Child – Adult Survivors of War*. Our group of men and women from Peru, Colombia, Kurdistan, Iraq and Kuwait were invited to present at *Peace One Day* at City Hall, Bristol, in 2013. It meant a lot to me when a British man from the audience came to me to say he understood our experiences. It was during the project and after speaking to an audience of 250 people, I felt as if a mountain had lifted off my back. After that, my sister and friends wanted to find a place to share their stories with Rissa. I got more involved in co-producing *Under the Shade of a Tree – Somali Women Speak*, helping to gather women who had been through war and sought refuge and safety; their narratives reflected the emotional impact war has on women.

In the West, meetings are generally taken around a table.

However, in Somalia, conflicts – whether tribal or otherwise – are traditionally resolved by meeting under a tree, and tribal leaders and elders are the ones to resolve conflicts.

The name of this book is symbolic not only as a reflection of the practice of meeting under the shade of a tree, but also because trees provided safety when the women needed to seek refuge in faraway cities, and shade from the sweltering heat on their journeys.

I have attended the Trauma Awareness Training, and it helped me to understand what happened to me when I left my family in Moscow to travel to the Netherlands. For six months, I couldn't feel my feet on the ground, which I now know is a trauma response. I remember seeing my sister for the first time when she arrived in the Netherlands. I could feel the ground under my feet, as if I had landed.

I worked with Bushara Somali women's group from 2000, but in 2013 I decided to set up Heroes as a multiethnic group of women who meet and do activities. This has helped me with my work in the refugee community and also leading Heroes Group, where sometimes women can be triggered by past memories. I can reassure them with what I learnt from the training, for example how to bring them back to present by saying the date and year.

Heroes Group honours the Mother; she is like sugar, the person who makes the home sweet, the nurturing part of our lives. We miss her if she is not there.

3. Rissa Mohabir

Under the Shade of the Tree
Somali Women Speak.

The art of oral poetry
Their message
A collective memory
Of shared experiences.

War fractures families
Clans and communities
Living as refugees
In exile.

Somali Women Speak
From the heart
To build bridges
To promote peace.

This is a story with no full
stop ... until war ends